SOUND WAVES 1

NATIONAL EDITION

BARBARA MURRAY
TERRI WATSON

firefly education

Use the Access Code provided by your teacher to log into **www.soundwaveskids.com.au**.
You will need this code to access the online learning resources.

My Access Code is: _____

Teachers: For detailed instructions on how to obtain your class Access Code for the year,
go to **www.soundwavesonline.com.au** or contact Firefly Education.

Illustrations by Chris Dent, Creative Design Studios, Eudlo, Qld
Cover by Cassie Nelson
Designed by Joanne Morgan

First edition published 2010
Reprinted with corrections 2011 (twice), 2012, 2013, 2014, 2015, 2016 (twice), 2017, 2018

Firefly Education Pty Ltd
PO Box 634, Buderim, Qld 4556 Australia
Tel: +61 7 5445 5749 Fax: (07) 5445 5171
Email: info@fireflyeducation.com.au
www.fireflyeducation.com.au

National Library of Australia
ISBN 978 1 74135 156 9

Printed in China.

MIX
Paper from
responsible sources
FSC® C074595

ontents

WELCOME TO SOUND WAVES

Sound Waves is a word study program designed to develop reading, spelling and writing skills through phonemic awareness. Phonemic awareness is essentially a knowledge and understanding of the sounds and sound patterns of our language.

What is the Sound Waves Approach?

The Sound Waves approach uses a sound-to-letter strategy, which acknowledges that sounds can be represented in more than one way. The Sound Waves approach focuses first on the basic units of sound in our language – phonemes. It then explores the letters that represent these sounds and how they can be put together to form the words in our language.

The phonemic approach to learning our language is essential because it replaces rote learning with strategies for reading and writing. It incorporates explicit teaching and game-based learning activities.

Before getting into Sound Waves, you'll need to understand two key terms:

Phoneme: A phoneme is the smallest unit of sound in a word.

Grapheme: A grapheme is the letter or letter combination used to represent a phoneme in written form.

QUESTIONS YOU MAY ASK

Can one grapheme represent more than one sound?

YES! The grapheme **x** can represent the blend of two sounds, [k c q ck x(ks)] [s ss se x(ks) c] as in *fox* – [f ff] [o a] [k c q ck x(ks)] [s ss se x(ks) c]. It is included in both [k c q ck x(ks)] and [s ss se x(ks) c] units.

The letters **u**, **u_e**, **ue**, **eau**, **ew** are sometimes classed as single graphemes that can all represent the blend of two sounds, [y] [oo], for example: *music* [m mm] [y] [oo] [z zz s] [i] [k c q ck x(ks)].

This blend is introduced in Sound Waves 2 in both the [y] and [oo] units. If you are not sure if a (yoo) blend is present in a word, say the word aloud with the [oo] sound only, for example: *music* [m mm] [oo] [z zz s] [i] [k c q ck x(ks)].

What is a split digraph?

The split digraphs are: **a_e** as in *cake*, **e_e** as in *these*, **i_e** as in *ice-cream,* **o_e** as in *rose* and **u_e** as in *flute*. Sound Waves classes words with split digraphs when **one sound only** splits the **a**, **e**, **i**, **o** or **u** and the final **e**, for example: *stage* but not *change*.

What is the schwa?

The **er** in *ladder* is not the same as the **er** in *her*. It is called the schwa sound. It is similar to the **u** in *cup* but softer. It is the sound of the **a** in *final*, the **e** in *bucket*, the **i** in *dolphin*, the **o** in *iron* and the **u** in *cactus*.

What about blends?

Common blends, such as **bl**, **cr** and **sn** are each two separate graphemes representing two separate sounds.

Similarly, blends like **spr**, **spl** and **scr** are each three separate graphemes representing three separate sounds.

Letters **al**, **el**, **il**, **ol**, **ul**, **le** can all be two separate graphemes representing the blend of two sounds – [er] [l ll]. For example: *moral*, *label*, *pencil*, *petrol*, *consul*, *table*.

The letters **qu** can also work as two separate graphemes representing the blend of two separate sounds – [k c q ck x(ks)] [w wh u], as in *quit*. Thus the grapheme **q** is in the [k c q ck x(ks)] unit and the grapheme **u** is in the [w wh u] unit.

The Sound Waves Program contains 36 sound units designed to fit neatly into a school year. Each sound unit is built on a 3-step process to be taught within a single week. This 3-step teaching program has been tailored to complement the Student Book activities for each sound unit.

For more detail on the Suggested Weekly Program, please refer to *Sound Waves 1 Teacher Book*.

STEP 1

MONDAY

Explore the Sound

Warm Up – Engage students and focus their attention on phonemes and graphemes.

Identify the Sound – Introduce the focus sound for the week.

Chant & Action – Consolidate phonemic awareness orally, aurally and kinaesthetically.

Brainstorm – Explore and record words that contain the focus sound.

Sound Waves Teaching Chart – Discuss the sound box for the focus sound.

Explore the List Words

List Words – Read through the List Words for the week with students.

Games and Activities – Consolidate student understanding of the List Words and their meanings.

Set Home Study Tasks – A variety of homework tasks can be found in the *Sound Waves 1 Teacher Book*.

STEP 2

TUESDAY–THURSDAY

Working with Words

Focus Concepts – Explicitly teach any new or difficult concepts.

Student Book Activities – Guide students through the activities.

Play Great Games – Use games to consolidate and reinforce the content of the unit.

Art Activities – Create art related to the icon and phoneme.

STEP 3

FRIDAY

Mark and Discuss

Mark and Discuss – Go over remaining Student Book activities with the class.

Review – Ensure students are familiar with the List Words and words on the brainstormed lists.

Getting Started

Teacher's Notes

Activity 1

Discuss with students that words are made up of sounds.

Have students identify the initial sound in their names.

Identify the initial sound in the animals' names in Activity 1.

Have students identify the final sound of each animal name.

Students complete Activity 1.

After completing Activity 1, have students identify pairs of animals that start with the same sound, excluding those starting with **s d dd**.

Activity 2

Ask students to look at the large sound box in Activity 2.

Discuss and explain:
- the icon is the picture that represents the sound (phoneme)
- the letters show different ways to write the sound in a word (graphemes)
- the other pictures and words are examples of words with these graphemes.

Activity 3

Have students identify the sound for each sound box in Activity 3 by:
- saying the icon name
- saying the sound represented by the first grapheme in the sound box.

With students, turn to other pages in the book and identify the sounds represented by other sound boxes. Turn to pages 78 and 79. Say all the consonant and vowel sounds.

1 **What** is the sound at the start of 🦆?
Colour all of the animals that start with this sound.

2 In Sound Waves we use sound boxes to represent the sounds.

Large Sound Box

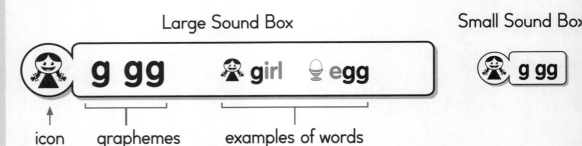

icon ↑   graphemes (spelling choices)   examples of words with these graphemes

Small Sound Box

3 **Say** the sound for these sound boxes.

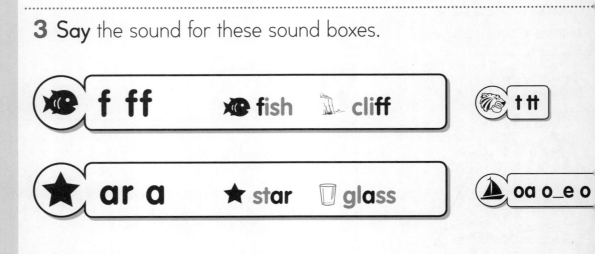

Say the sounds for these blend boxes. **Match** the boxes to the pictures.

 br    cl

---

Say the name of the animal. **Write** a stroke on the line for each sound in the name.

Find some healthy food.

Colour the shape **green** if the picture name has **four** sounds.
Colour the shape **red** if you hear 🍎 a in the picture name.
Colour the shape **yellow** if you hear 🔔 b bb in the picture name.

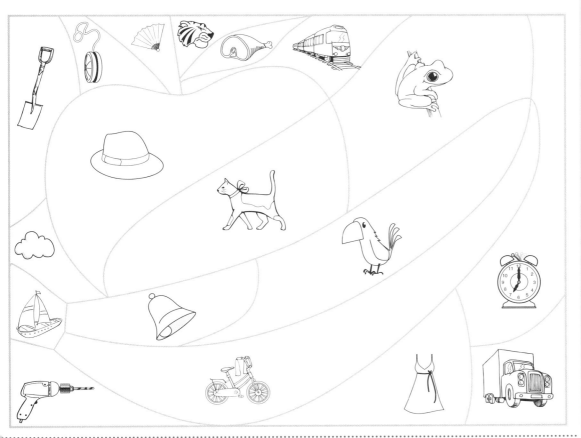

Teacher's Notes

Activity 4

These boxes are used to represent a blend of two sounds.

Have students identify the blends in Activity 4.

Next, turn to page 25 and find two boxes like these. Identify the blend for each.

Students complete Activity 4.

Activity 5

Say the animal names in Activity 5 with students. Segment the names into sounds, for example /d/u/ck/, /f/i/sh/. With students, write a stroke for each sound as they say it, for example *duck* III, *fish* III.

Next, have students segment their own names into sounds.

Activity 6

Direct the students to the pictures in Activity 6.

Have students:

• identify the initial sound of each picture name

• identify the final sound of each picture name

• segment and count the number of sounds in each picture name, for example /b/e/ll/ – 3. Have students hold up a finger for each sound.

To complete Activity 6:

• have students identify all of the four sound pictures and colour these parts green

• next have students identify all of the 🍎 a pictures and colour these parts red

• Finally, have students identify all of the 🔔 b bb pictures and colour these parts yellow.

For more introductory activities for Sound Waves 1 see the *Sound Waves 1 Teacher Book*.

 **b bb**    balloon   ribbon

List Words

bat	bed	brick	black
bug	ball	bring	blue
bell	sob	brush	rubbing
big	rub	block	cubby

Letters   Words

1 **Underline** the letter or letters for  b bb in each List Word. If any of these are not in the sound box, write them with a word example in the box above.

2 **Colour** the balloon if you hear b bb in the picture name.

3 **Write** b to finish the words. **Join** the words to the pictures.

 ___ug   ___at   ___ed   ___ell   so___

Write b, bb or B to finish the words.
Draw pictures in the balloons to match the words.

★ We usually write **b** for **b bb**. Sometimes we write **bb** in the middle of a word. **B** starts sentences and the names of people and places.

Write b.	Write bb.	Write B.
a __ig __all	cu__y	__en

Colour the picture if you hear br **at the start of the picture name.**

 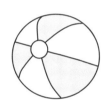 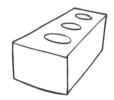 

Colour the picture if you hear bl **at the start of the picture name.**

Write br **or** bl **to finish the word for the picture.**

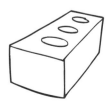  

____ick   ____ack   ____ock   ____ush

For the Extra Challenge turn to page 82. ISBN 978 1 74135 156 9

 a  apple

List Words

at	Dad	sat	and
am	bad	bat	that
an	had	hand	have
man	has	back	family

Letters | Words

Letters	Words

1 Underline the letter or letters for  a in each List Word. If any of these are not in the sound box, write them with a word example in the box above.

2 Colour the apple **red** if you hear  a in the picture name.

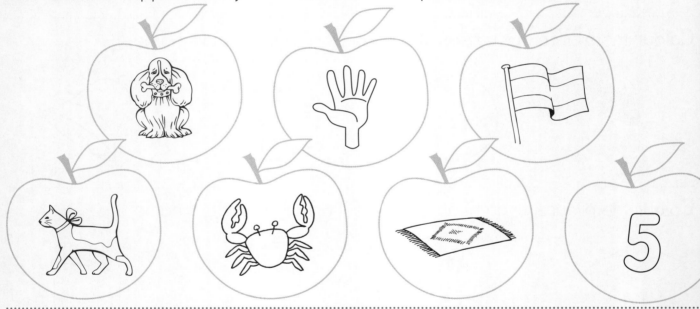

3 Write words to rhyme in the apples.

man

____an
____an

had

____ad
____ad

bat

____at
____at

Circle the correct word to finish the sentence. **Draw** a picture for each sentence.

I have a sat. / hat.

She has a bat. / that.

He has an / am apple.

This is my have. / family.

Make real words with the letters in the apples.

l, b, th — at

h, s, p — and

b, g, bl — ack

Read the words. **Cross** out the ones that don't make sense.
Colour the apples with the real words.

at ag am af

had hat hab has have

For the Extra Challenge turn to page 82.
ISBN 978 1 74135 156 9

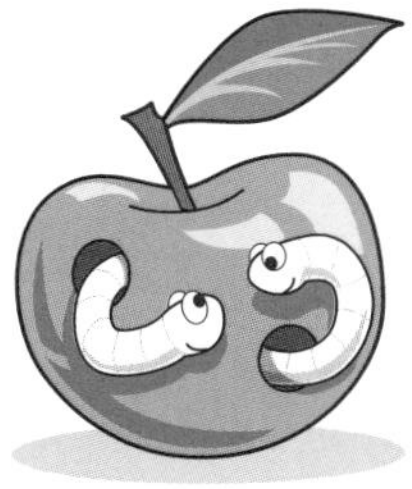

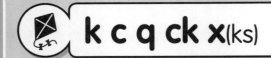 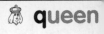
List Words

cap	king	clip	box
cut	kiss	clock	six
can	kick	cross	quick
cat	lock	crack	quack

Letters   **Words**

1 Underline the letter or letters for **kcqckx**(ks) in each List Word. If any of these are not in the sound box, write them with a word example in the box above.

2 Colour the triangle **blue** if you hear **kcqckx**(ks) at the **start** of the picture name.

3 Colour the triangle **yellow** if you hear **kcqckx**(ks) at the **end** of the picture name.

4 Finish the words to match the pictures.

 c__p

 c__t

 __an

king __ing

 k__ss

Write **cl** to finish the words. **Join** the pictures to the correct words.

____ap

____ock

____ip

____ub

6 Write **cr** to finish the words. **Join** the pictures to the correct words.

____ab

✚

____ack

____ash

____oss

Write **qu** or **cl** to finish the words. **Join** the pictures to the correct words.

____ick

____ock

____ick

____een

8 Write **qu** or **cr** to finish the words. **Join** the pictures to the correct words.

____ilt

____ack

____op

____ack

Look at the pictures. **Write ck** or **x** to finish the picture names.

ki____   si____   lo____   bo____   su____

0 **Read** the words. **Underline** the letters that make the 🔊 **k c q ck x**(ks) sound. **Draw** the pictures.

six black cats	a clock on a box	a cup with a crack

For the Extra Challenge turn to page 82.

Unit 5

e   egg

List Words

get	egg	went	said
men	end	best	any
red	tell	neck	seven
ten	when	help	head

Letters   Words

Letters	Words

1 Underline the letter or letters for ⬤e in each List Word. If any of these are not in the sound box, write them with a word example in the box above.

2 Colour the egg if you hear ⬤e in the picture name.

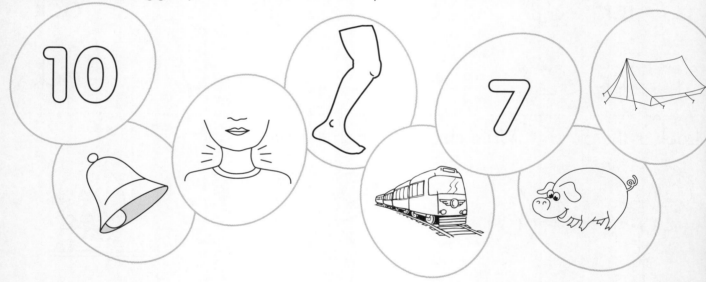

3 Write words to rhyme in the eggs.

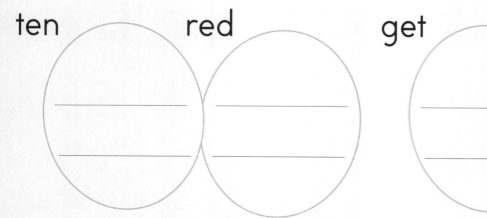

ten   red   get   bell

Make real words by joining the letters in the eggs to the endings.

end	est	ent

_____   _____   _____

_____   _____   _____

_____   _____   _____

Read the words. **Cross** out the ones that don't make sense.

then	shen	when	best	yest	test
neck	geck	peck	help	jelp	yelp

Write the letters for the sound to finish the words. **Use** e, ea, ai or a.

n___ck   wh___n   s___d   h___d

___ny   h___lp   w___nt   s___ven

Arrange the letters in the eggs to make words.

m n e   g e g   d n e   n y a

_____   _____   _____   _____

a d i s   d e h a   n h e w   p l h e

s_____   h_____   w_____   h_____

For the Extra Challenge turn to page 82.

Unit 6

 **d dd**  duck ✎ paddle

List Words

Dad	and	drop	Daddy
dog	sand	drill	ladder
sad	lend	dress	door
duck	send	drum	friend

Letters   Words

Letters	Words

1 **Underline** the letter or letters for  d dd in each List Word. If any of these are not in the sound box, write them with a word example in the box above.

2 **Colour** the duck if you hear d dd at the **start** of the picture name.

3 **Colour** the duck if you hear d dd at the **end** of the picture name.

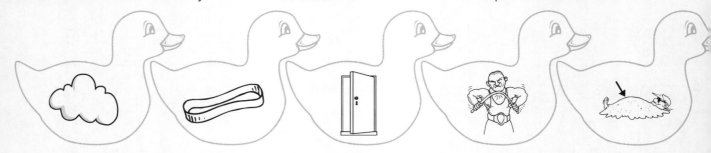

4 **Finish** the words to match the pictures.

D____d   ____og   li____   du____   sa____

Write d, dd or **D** to finish the words.
Draw pictures in the ducks to match the words.
★ We usually write **d** for 🦆 d dd . Sometimes we write **dd** in the
   middle of a word. **D** starts sentences and the names of people and places.

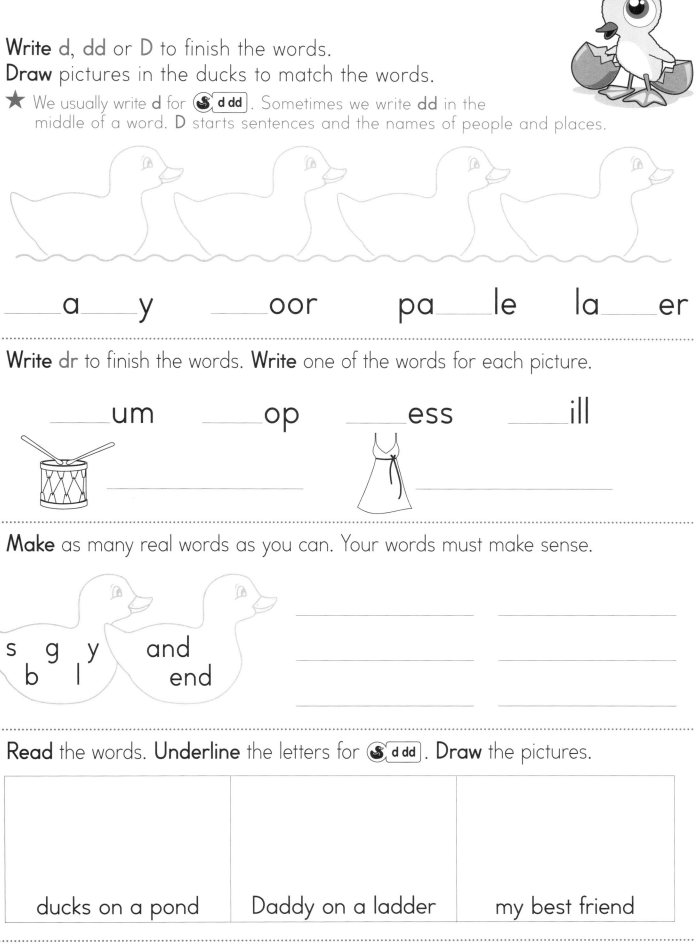

___a___y   ___oor   pa___le   la___er

Write dr to finish the words. **Write** one of the words for each picture.

___um   ___op   ___ess   ___ill

_____   _____

Make as many real words as you can. Your words must make sense.

s g y   and
 b l   end

_____   _____

_____   _____

_____   _____

Read the words. **Underline** the letters for 🦆 d dd . **Draw** the pictures.

ducks on a pond	Daddy on a ladder	my best friend

 **i**  **igloo**

List Words

it	his	ship	which
is	win	fish	give
in	will	pick	live
did	this	sing	little

Letters   Words

1 **Underline** the letter or letters for  **i** in each List Word. If any of these are not in the sound box, write them with a word example in the box above.

2 Colour the igloo if you hear  **i** in the picture name.

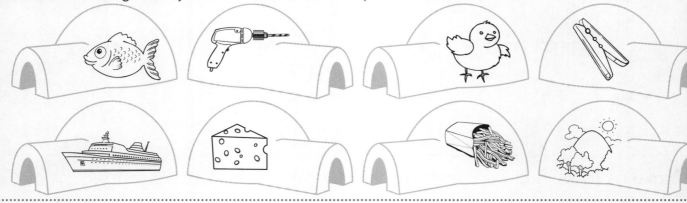

3 Write words to rhyme in the igloos.

it

in

big

hill

Make real words with the letters in the igloos.

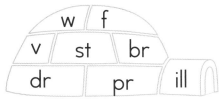
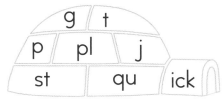

_____ _____ _____

_____ _____ _____

_____ _____ _____

_____ _____ _____

Circle the correct word to finish the sentence. **Draw** a picture for each sentence.

Did you pick this   sing?
                     ring?

I live on this   ship.
                  little.

Write answers to the questions. **Colour** all the words with  i .

Did she hit or miss? _____

Did he trip or skip? _____

Is his fish big or little? _____

Is her fish big or little? _____

List Words

if	fun	frog	left
off	fill	from	soft
fat	fell	flat	puffed
fog	fix	flag	after

Letters   Words

1 **Underline** the letter or letters for f ff in each List Word. If any of these are not in the sound box, write them with a word example in the box above.

2 **Colour** the fish if you hear f ff in the picture name.

3 **Write** a, e, i, o or u to make f ff words.

f__ll

f__ll

f__t

f__t

f__n

f__n

f__x

f__x

__f

__ff

Write f, ff or F to finish the words.
Draw a picture inside the fish for each word.

★ We usually write **f** for 🐟 **f ff**. Sometimes we write **ff** in the middle of a word or at the end. **F** starts sentences and the names of people and places.

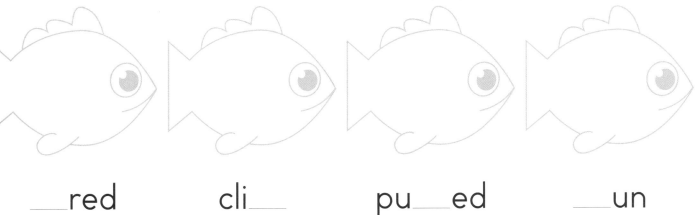

__red   cli__   pu__ed   __un

Write fl to finish the words. **Join** the pictures to the correct words.

____at   ____op

____ag   ____ower

6 Write fr to finish the words. **Join** the pictures to the correct words.

____om   ____og

____esh   ____uit

Write ft to finish the words. **Write** one of these words for each picture.

li____   le____   so____   a____er

Read the words. **Cross** out the ones that don't make sense.

frog	frol	from	flag	flaf	flat
lift	left	laft	huffed	puffed	guffed

For the Extra Challenge turn to page 82.   ISBN 978 1 74135 156 9

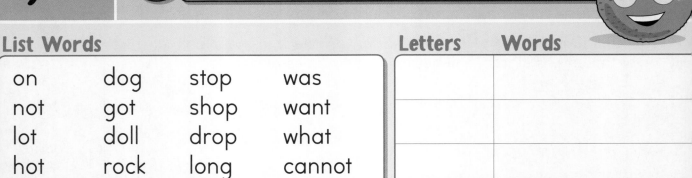

Unit 9

 o a   **orange**   **watch**

List Words

on	dog	stop	was
not	got	shop	want
lot	doll	drop	what
hot	rock	long	cannot

Letters	Words

1 **Underline** the letter or letters for **o a** in each List Word. If any of these are not in the sound box, write them with a word example in the box above.

2 **Colour** the orange slice **orange** if you hear **o a** in the picture name. **Write** a stroke on the line for each sound in the picture name, like this: *sock /s/o/ck/* **III**.

III ___

3 **Write** words to rhyme in the oranges.

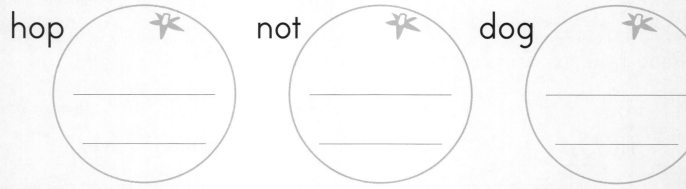

hop   not   dog

Make real words with the letters in the orange trees.

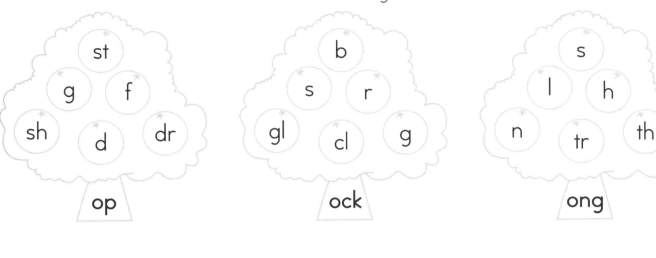

Tree 1 letters: st, g, f, sh, d, dr — base: **op**

Tree 2 letters: b, s, r, gl, cl, g — base: **ock**

Tree 3 letters: s, l, h, n, tr, th — base: **ong**

_____   _____   _____

_____   _____   _____

_____   _____   _____

Write the letter **a** in the words in the box. **Finish** the sentences with these words.

★ We sometimes write **a** for  o a , as in w**a**tch.

w___s	_____ did you drop?
w___nt	I _____ on the rock.
Wh___t	I _____ a long hotdog.

Read the words. **Rearrange** the letters to make new words.

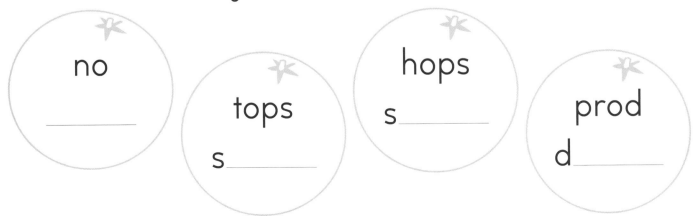

no _____

tops s_____

hops s_____

prod d_____

For the Extra Challenge turn to page 82.

 **g gg**    girl   egg

List Words

big	get	grab	good
bag	egg	grin	going
leg	hug	glad	hugged
rug	girl	glue	hugging

Letters   Words

1 **Underline** the letter or letters for 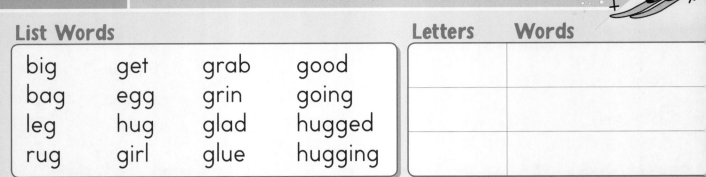 **g gg** in each List Word. If any of these are not in the sound box, write them with a word example in the box above.

2 **Colour** the gift if you hear **g gg** in the picture name. **Write** a stroke below the picture for each sound in the gift name, like this: *dog /d/o/g/* **III**.

III

3 **Write** words to rhyme in the boxes.

tag   peg   pig   bug

Write g, gg or G to finish the words. Read and draw the finished story.

★ We usually write **g** for ![g gg]. Sometimes we write **gg** in the middle of a word.
G starts sentences and the names of people and places.

_____abby is a _____irl.

She is _____oing to her do_____.

She is hu_____ing her do_____.

- -

Colour the gift if you hear gr at the **start** of the gift name.

- -

Colour the gift if you hear gl at the **start** of the gift name.

- -

Write gr or gl to finish the words. Write one of your words for each picture.

gr	_____ab	_____ad	_____in	_____ue
gl	_____ass	_____ass	_____ub	_____eet

_____

_____

_____

_____

For the Extra Challenge turn to page 82. ISBN 978 1 74135 156 9

u o 🌂 umbrella 🐵 monkey

List Words

up	run	must	come
us	cup	jump	some
but	drum	much	love
bus	shut	duck	done

Letters	Words

1 **Underline** the letter or letters for 🌂 **u o** in each List Word. If any of these are not in the sound box, write them with a word example in the box above.

2 **Colour** the section **blue** if you hear 🌂 **u o** in the picture name.
Colour the section **yellow** if you don't hear 🌂 **u o** in the picture name.

3 **Write** words to rhyme in the umbrellas.

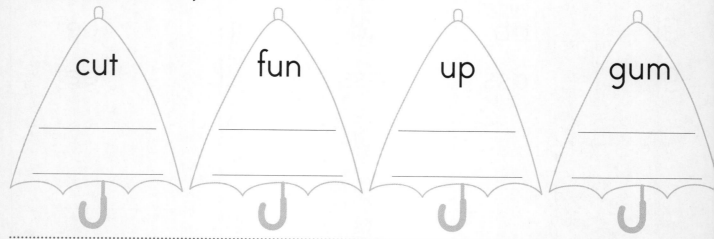

cut   fun   up   gum

Make real words with the letters in the umbrellas.

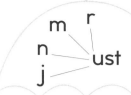
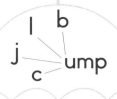

_____ _____ _____

_____ _____ _____

_____ _____ _____

Read the words. Cross out the ones that don't make sense.

up	ut	us	much	ruch	such
shut	plut	grut	drum	flum	plum

Write the letter o in the words in the box. Finish the sentences with these words.

★ We sometimes write o for ☂ u o , as in monkey 🐵.

C__me	Have you _____ the jobs?
s__me	_____ to the bus.
d__ne	I _____ my pup.
l__ve	He has _____ cups for us.

Finish the words to match the clues.

c _____   b _____   b _____   _____ um

For the Extra Challenge turn to page 82. ISBN 978 1 74135 156 9

 **h** 🏠 **house**

List Words

him	hill	here	have
hit	home	who	having

Letters   Words

1 Underline the letter or letters for 🏠 h in each List Word. If any of these are not in the sound box, write them with a word example in the box above.

2 Colour the house if you hear 🏠 h in the picture name. **Draw** a chimney on the house for each sound in the picture name. The first one is done for you.

3 Make as many words as you can. Your words must make sense.

h | ill op od
ig im it

_____

_____

4 Write h or H to finish the words. **Join** the sentences to the pictures.

____ere is my ____ome.

We are ____aving fun.

Who is the boy on the ____ill?

j  **jellyfish**

st Words			
am	jug	just	jumped
et	job	jump	jumping

Letters	Words

Underline the letter or letters for [j] in each List Word. If any of these are not in the sound box, write them with a word example in the box above.

Colour the jellyfish if you hear [j] in the picture name.
Draw a tentacle on the jellyfish for each sound you hear in the picture name.

Make as many words as you can. Your words must make sense.

j

et
ob ip
ug am

_____ _____

_____ _____

Write the letter j in the words in the box. **Finish** the sentences with these words.

____ump   Jim can _____.

____umping   He _____ over the jug.

____umped   He is _____.

For the Extra Challenge turn to page 82. ISBN 978 1 74135 156 9

ai ay a_e snail hay cake

List Words

day	take	name	rain
say	make	game	they
may	cake	same	eight
play	made	place	today

Letters   Words

1 **Underline** the letter or letters for **ai ay a_e** in each List Word. If any of these are not in the sound box, write them with a word example in the box above.

2 **Colour** the things in the picture if you hear **ai ay a_e** in the picture name.

3 **Make** real **ay** words with the letters in the snail.

★ We sometimes write **ay** for **ai ay a_e**, as in h**ay** .

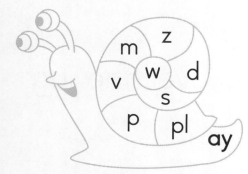

pay

Write a_e to finish the words. **Join** the pictures to the correct words.

★ We sometimes write a_e for 🐌 ai ay a_e , as in c**a**k**e** 🎂.

___m___   g___m___   c___k___   m___d___

___m___   g___t___   r___k___   pl___c___

Read the words on the snails. **Cross** out the ones that don't make sense.

pay   may
tay   way

came   same
rame   name

gate   late
jate   mate

make   dake
take   cake

Finish the sentences with the words in the brackets.
Colour all the 🐌 ai ay a_e words.

_____ will stay for _____ days. | eight |
                                                    | They |

_____ we had some _____ . | rain |
                                                    | Today |

Make a coloured trail for each snail. **Finish** the words with ay, a_e or ai.
Colour ay stones **blue**. **Colour** a_e stones **yellow**. **Colour** ai stones **red**.
Colour the snails to match their trails.

s___   t___k___   m___d___   n___l___   t___l

c___k___   m___   sn___l   g___m___   pl___

r___n   tr___n   p___   d___   g___v___

Unit 14

 l ll    lizard   bell

List Words				Letters	Words
fell	help	glad	leaf		
well	milk	flat	look		
will	belt	blend	live		
ball	cold	cliff	quilt		

1 **Underline** the letter or letters for l ll in each List Word. If any of these are not in the sound box, write them with a word example in the box above.

2 **Colour** the picture if you hear l ll in the picture name.
Colour one 🍃 for each sound you hear in the picture name.

            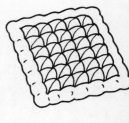

3 **Write** **bl** or **gl** to finish the words. **Write** one of the words for each picture.

bl
gl

___ad   ___end   ___oss   ___ock

4 **Write** **cl** or **fl** to finish the words. **Write** one of the words for each picture.

cl
fl

___am   ___at   ___iff   ___ake

Write **I**, **II** or **L** to finish the words. **Draw** the picture.

★ We usually write I for . Sometimes we write **II** in the middle of a word or at the end. **L** starts sentences and the names of people and places.

___izards ___ike ___o___ipops.

Read the words in the leaves. **Cross** out the ones that don't make sense.
Write a word from each leaf for the picture beside it.

hill
rill
will  _____

fell
bell
vell  _____

tall
dall
ball  _____

cold
sold
vold  _____

milk
dilk
silk  _____

gelt
belt
melt  _____

yelp
help
telp  _____

elf
self
nelf  _____

tilt
dilt
quilt _____

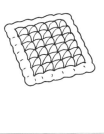

Arrange the letters in the leaves to make List Words.

_____ _____ _____ _____

For the Extra Challenge turn to page 82. ISBN 978 1 74135 156 9

 **ee e ea**   **bee**   **me**  **seat**

List Words

me	she	sea	three
be	see	eat	beach
we	been	each	any
he	tree	read	many

Letters **Words**

1 **Underline** the letter or letters for **ee e ea** in each List Word. If any of these are not in the sound box, write them with a word example in the box above.

2 **Colour** the picture if you hear **ee e ea** in the picture name.
Colour one 🐝 for each sound you hear in the picture name.

3 **Write ee** to finish the words. **Join** the pictures to the correct words.
★ We sometimes write **ee** for **ee e ea**, as in b**ee** 🐝.

s____   tr____   m__t   3   b__n

b____   f__d   f__t   thr____

4 **Write ea** to finish the words. **Join** the pictures to the correct words.
★ We sometimes write **ea** for **ee e ea**, as in s**ea**t.

t____   ____t   l__f   r__d

s____   s__t   m__t   ____ch

Read the words on the beehives.
Cross out the ones that don't make sense.

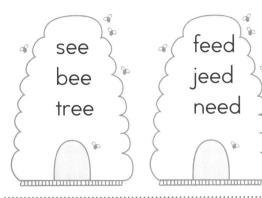

see	feed	deep	been	deat
bee	jeed	feep	neen	meat
tree	need	keep	green	neat

Write the letters for ee e ea to finish the words. **Use** e, ee, ea or y.
Write one of the words for each picture.

m____   ____t   an____   thr____   man____

h____   sh____   tr____   b____ch   ____ch

_____   3 _____   _____

Say the words. **Colour yellow** if you hear ee e ea.
Colour blue if you don't hear ee e ea.

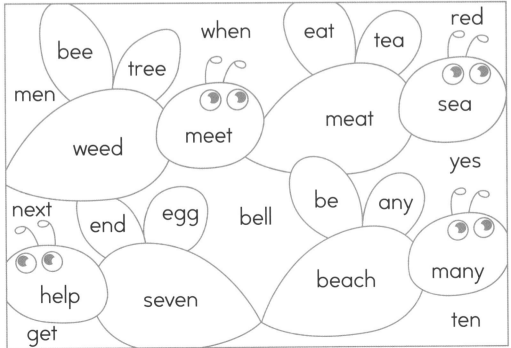

when eat tea red
bee tree men meet meat sea
weed yes
next egg bell be any
end beach many
help seven ten
get

For the Extra Challenge turn to page 82.   ISBN 978 1 74135 156 9

 **m mm**    moon   hammer

List Words

Mum	camp	smash	Mummy
man	jump	smile	swimming
men	pump	smell	hummed
made	stamp	small	humming

Letters   Words

1 **Underline** the letter or letters for m mm in each List Word. If any of these are not in the sound box, write them with a word example in the box above.

2 **Colour** the moon if you hear m mm in the picture name.
Count the sounds in each picture name. **Write** this number in the star.

3 **Write** m, mm or M to finish the words. **Draw** the pictures.

★ We usually write **m** for m mm. Sometimes we write **mm** in the middle of a word. **M** starts sentences and the names of people and places.

The ___an ___ade a ___at.

___u___y is swi___ing.

Colour the moon **yellow** if you hear `sm` at the **start** of the picture name.
Colour the moon **blue** if you hear `mp` at the **end** of the picture name.

Write **sm** or **mp** to finish the words. **Join** the words to the pictures.

___ell   ___ile   ca___   pu___

___ash   ___all   ju___   sta___

Write **m** or **mm** in the words in the box. **Finish** the sentences with these words.

hu___

hu___ing

hu___ed

Mummy is _____.

I can _____.

The men _____ too.

Read the words. **Cross** out the ones that don't make sense.

man	make	jump	camp
min	made	fump	lamp
men	mate	lump	samp
mun	mabe	pump	stamp

For the Extra Challenge turn to page 82.

List Words

by	like	five	find
my	ride	nine	light
cry	side	fine	right
fly	time	nice	while

Letters	Words

1 Underline the letter or letters for  i_e y in each List Word. If any of these are not in the sound box, write them with a word example in the box above.

2 Colour the picture if you hear  i_e y in the picture name.
Colour one 🍦 for each sound you hear in the picture name.

3 Make real words with the letters in the ice-creams.
Finish the sentences with these words.
★ We sometimes write **y** for  i_e y, as in fly 🪰.

b c m
y

cr dr tr gr
y

wh fl ch sh
y

_____ dad had a _____ on his head.

_____ did the boy start to _____ ?

Write i_e to finish the words. **Join** the pictures to the correct words.

★ We sometimes write i_e for (i_e y), as in ice-cream.

r__d__   t__m__   f__v__   5 n__n__

s__d__   l__k__   n__c__   9 wh__l__

Read the words. **Cross** out the ones that don't make sense.

try	bry	nine	mine	ride	fide	kind	gind
cry	gry	bine	line	wide	side	tind	mind
fry	dry	fine	gine	kide	tide	find	hind

Make real words with the letters in the ice-creams.

m n r h
ice
_____
_____

p n r w
ipe
_____
_____

l b bl sp
ike
_____
_____

m l p r
ight
_____
_____

For the Extra Challenge turn to page 82.   ISBN 978 1 74135 156 9

 **n nn** **net**  **winner**

List Words

can	snap	snack	dinner
sun	snip	snake	cannot

Letters   Words

1 **Underline** the letter or letters for n nn in each List Word. If any of these are not in the sound box, write them with a word example in the box above.

2 **Colour** the net if you hear n nn in the picture name. **Count** the sounds in each picture name. **Write** this number in the handle of the net.

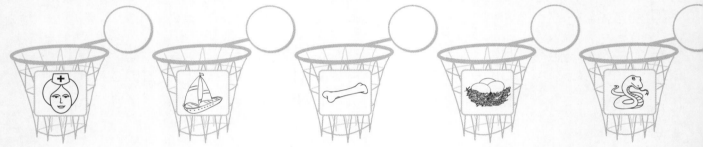

3 **Finish** the words to match the pictures.

s___n   c___n   s___ip   sna___e   di___er

4 **Write** sn to finish the words in the box. **Finish** the sentences with these words

___ap
___ack
___ake

I cannot _____ my fingers.

The _____ is in the sun.

Mum gave me a _____.

ist Words

ring	sing	song	king
rang	sang	sung	long

Letters **Words**

Underline the letter or letters for 💍 ng in each List Word. If any of these are not in the sound box, write them with a word example in the box above.

Colour the ring if you hear 💍 ng in the picture name. **Count** the sounds in each picture name. **Write** this number in the circle.

Write ng to finish the words. **Draw** the picture.

I ra____ the bell for the ki____.

Then he sa____ a lo____ so____.

Write words to rhyme in the rings.

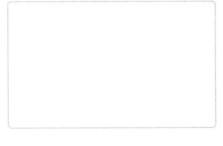

ring   sang   long

____   ____   ____

For the Extra Challenge turn to page 82.

oa o_e o   ⛵ boat   🌹 rose   comb

List Words

go	old	home	road
no	cold	nose	boat
so	told	rode	goes
going	hold	also	know

Letters   Words

1 Underline the letter or letters for ⛵ oa o_e o in each List Word. If any of these are not in the sound box, write them with a word example in the box above.

2 Colour the boat if you hear ⛵ oa o_e o in the picture name.
Count the sounds in each picture name. **Write** this number in the smoke.

3 Colour the letter or letters for ⛵ oa o_e o in the words in the box.
Finish the sentences with these words.

go
goes
going

He will _____ on the road.
She _____ on the boat.
We are _____ home.

4 Write o_e to finish the words. **Join** the pictures to the correct words.
★ We sometimes write o_e for ⛵ oa o_e o, as in r o se 🌹.

n _ t _   r _ s _   r _ p _   n _ s _

b _ n _   r _ d _   h _ m _   th _ s _

Make real words with the letters in the boats.

g n t s — old

r f h c — ope

r n k h — ose

j sp w l — oke

_____ _____ _____ _____

_____ _____ _____ _____

_____ _____ _____ _____

Finish the sentences with the words in the brackets.
Colour all the  oa o_e o words **yellow**.

I _____ there will be _____ rain today. | no / know |

He _____ his bike on the _____ . | rode / road |

She _____ that her _____ is red. | knows / nose |

Read the words. **Cross** out the ones that don't make sense.

nose	vose	hose	rose	those	close
bone	sone	cone	pone	brone	stone
cold	hold	nold	fold	told	zold

Finish the words with a_e, i_e or o_e.
Colour a_e parts **yellow**, i_e parts **red** and o_e parts **green**.

h_m_   r_k_   w_p_   h_p_   g_m_

s_d_   n_s_   h_t_   h_d_

For the Extra Challenge turn to page 82. ISBN 978 1 74135 156 9

p pp  **pig** slipper

List Words

pram	plan	spill	kept
press	plane	speak	puppy

Letters	Words

1 Underline the letter or letters for 🐷 p pp in each List Word. If any of these are not in the sound box, write them with a word example in the box above.

2 Colour the pig if you hear 🐷 p pp in the picture name. **Write** a stroke below the pig for each sound in the picture name, like this: *shop |sh|o|p|* III.

3 Write p, pp or P to finish the words. **Draw** the picture.

★ We usually write **p** for 🐷 p pp . Sometimes we write **pp** in the middle of a word. **P** starts sentences and the names of people and places.

_____am has a _____ig and a _____u_____y.

4 Write the letters that are in the pigs to finish the words.
Write a word to match the clue.

pig			clue	
pl	_____an	_____ane	It can fly.	_____
pr	_____am	_____ess	push down	_____
sp	_____ill	_____eak	to talk	_____
pt	ke_____	we_____	did keep	_____

Letters	Words

List Words

rock	rake	ride	sorry
ring	read	rode	carry

Underline the letter or letters for r rr in each List Word. If any of these are not in the sound box, write them with a word example in the box above.

Where do you hear r rr in the picture name? **Colour** the robot **red** if it is **first** and **green** if it is **third**. **Finish** the words to match the pictures.

ro____   ch__rry   ____ing   ferr____   ra__e

Write r, rr or R to finish the words. **Draw** the picture.

★ We usually write **r** for r rr. Sometimes we write **rr** in the middle of a word. R starts sentences and the names of people and places.

____obby can ca____y the ____ock.

Write the letters that are in the robots to finish the words.
Write a word to match each clue.

r	____ock ____ide	go on a bike _____
	____ead ____ode	look at a book _____

rr	ca____y so____y	Bring it. _____
	be____y hu____y	Be quick! _____

For the Extra Challenge turn to page 83.

★ ar a   ★ star   🥛 glass

List Words

are	arm	card	ask
car	art	part	after
far	farm	park	last
bar	star	bark	fast

Letters   Words

1 Underline the letter or letters for ★ ar a in each List Word. If any of these are not in the sound box, write them with a word example in the box above.

2 Colour the picture if you hear ★ ar a in the picture name.

3 Write ar to finish the words. **Join** the pictures to the correct words.

★ We sometimes write **ar** for ★ ar a, as in st**ar** ★.

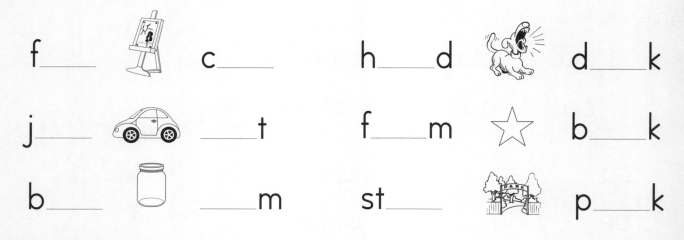

f___   c___   h___d   d___k

j___   ___t   f___m   b___k

b___   ___m   st___   p___k

Write Are to start each question. **Answer** the questions with **yes** or **no**.

_____ you a girl? _____

_____ you a boy? _____

_____ you a fast car? _____

_____ you part of a class? _____

_____ there sharks on a farm? _____

Make real words with the letters in the stars.

w
p
d   ark
sh
ch

c
d
h   ard
n
y

p
d
l   ast
g
f

_____   _____   _____

_____   _____   _____

_____   _____   _____

Say the words.

Colour yellow if you hear ⭐ ar a .

Colour blue if you don't hear ⭐ ar a .

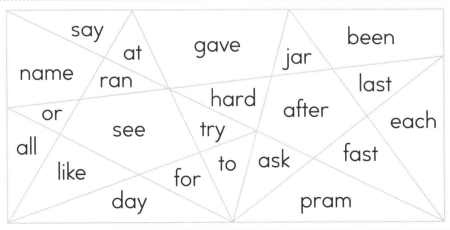

say
at   gave   been
name   jar
ran   last
or   hard   after
see   try   each
all
to   ask   fast
like   for
day   pram

For the Extra Challenge turn to page 83.   ISBN 978 1 74135 156 9

s ss se x(ks) c

🦭 **seal**   👥 **kiss**   🐁 **mouse**
🦊 **fox**   ✏️ **pencil**

List Words

miss	skip	scar	cents
missed	skate	scarf	said
missing	sleep	fox	mouse
cross	sling	fix	house

Letters	Words

1 **Underline** the letter or letters for 🦭 s ss se x(ks) c in each List Word. If any of these are not in the sound box, write them with a word example in the box above.

2 **Colour** the ball if you hear 🦭 s ss se x(ks) c in the picture name. **Count** the sounds in each picture name. **Write** this number in the seal.

3 **Write** the letters that are in the baskets to finish the words.
Finish the sentences with these words.

ss mi___ cro___	I can draw a _____.
se hou___ mou___	A _____ is under the desk.
c ___ents mi___e	It costs ten _____.

Write the letters that are in the baskets to finish the words.
Write a word to match the clue.

x	fi___ fo___	This is an animal. _____
sk	___ate ___ip	I jump with a rope. _____
sc	___arf ___ar	It keeps you warm. _____
sl	___eep ___ing	You do this at night. _____

Write s or ss in the words in the box. **Finish** the sentences with these words.

mi___
mi___es
mi___ed
___aid

Sometimes I _____ the bus.

Yesterday I _____ the bus.

Sam _____ that he _____

the bus every day.

Read the story. **Underline** the letters for (s ss se x(ks) c). **Draw** the picture.

Sid is a mouse.
He likes to skip and skate with
his friend the fox.
He sleeps on a scarf.

For the Extra Challenge turn to page 83.

 ir ur   **bird**    **nurse**

List Words

her	fur	first	were
stir	turn	third	work
girl	hurt	thirty	word
bird	surf	thirteen	circle

Letters   Words

1 Underline the letter or letters for ir ur in each List Word. If any of these are not in the sound box, write them with a word example in the box above.

2 Colour the bird if you hear ir ur in the picture name.
Give each bird one worm for each sound in the picture name.

3 Write ir to finish the words. **Join** the pictures to the correct words.
★ We sometimes write **ir** for ir ur , as in bird .

st____   b__d   th__d   30   sk____t

g____l   f__st   th__ty   sh____t

4 Finish these **ur** words.
★ We sometimes write **ur** for ir ur , as in nurse .

bur____   t____n   cur____

____ur____    hur____   ____urse

Write words from the brackets to finish the sentences.
Colour words with 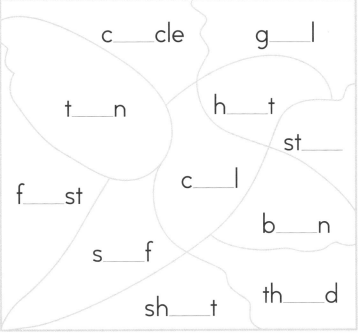 ir ur .

This _____ came _____.

The _____ were in a _____.

_____ girls went to _____.

There is a _____ on her _____.

[first girl]

[birds circle]

[work Thirty]

[shirt word]

Write letters for ir ur to finish the words. **Use** ir, ur, er, or or ere.
Write a word from the box to match each clue.

h____	s____f
f____	c____cle
w____k	w____
th____teen	

a shape _____

a number _____

at the beach _____

do a job _____

Write ir or ur to finish the words.
Colour ir parts **blue**.
Colour ur parts **purple**.

What can you see –
a **girl**,
a **shirt**
or
a **bird**?

Answer: _____

c____cle   g____l

t____n   h____t

st____

c____l

f____st   b____n

s____f   th____d

sh____t

For the Extra Challenge turn to page 83.   ISBN 978 1 74135 156 9

 **t tt**   **tiger**    **button**

List Words

tree	went	best	stay
try	want	lost	start
trap	tent	last	little
truck	bent	fast	better

Letters   Words

Letters	Words

1 **Underline** the letter or letters for  **tt** in each List Word. If any of these are not in the sound box, write them with a word example in the box above.

2 **Colour** the picture if you hear **tt** in the picture name. **Write** a stroke below the picture for each sound in the picture name, like this: *tree |t|r|ee|* **lll**.

_____   _____   _____   _____   _____

3 **Write** t, tt or T to finish the words. **Read** the sentences. **Draw** the picture.

★ We usually write **t** for  **t tt**. Sometimes we write **tt** in the middle of a word. T starts sentences and the names of people and places.

Li___le ___ommy ___iger is ___ro___ing on the ___rack. Li___le ___ommy ___iger is hun___ing for a snack.

Write st or tr to finish the words. Write one of your words for each picture.

st
tr

_____ee _____op _____ap _____ar

_____

_____

Write words to rhyme.

tent _____

best _____

last _____

Write the letters that are in the tigers to finish the words. Write a word to match each clue.

tr	_____ee _____y	a large plant _____
	_____ap _____uck	have a go _____
st	_____op be_____	get going _____
	_____art lo_____	can't find it _____
nt	we_____ wa_____	camp in it _____
	te_____ be_____	would like it _____

Count the sounds in the word in each tent. Write this number in the doorway. Colour the tents that have words with the same number of sounds.

trap   start   better   last   stay

 **or a**  horse   ball

List Words

all	or	corn	saw
ball	for	torn	your
tall	fork	horn	four
call	cork	more	because

Letters   Words

Letters	Words

1 **Underline** the letter or letters for  **or a** in each List Word. If any of these are not in the sound box, write them with a word example in the box above.

2 **Say** the name of each picture in the horse. **Colour** the parts **brown** if you hear **or a**.

3 **Write or** to finish the words. **Join** th pictures to the correct words.

★ We sometimes write **or** for **or a**, as in h**or**se.

c___n   h___n

t___n   b___n

c___k   p__k

f___k   w___n

4 **Colour** the letter or letters for **or a** in the words in the box. **Finish** the sentences with these words.

for	ball
Four	saw

We went _____ a walk.

We _____ a duck with a _____

_____ horses were eating corn.

Make real words with the letters in the horses.

b
d
t
sp
all

c
s
j
h
orn

c
g
f
n
ork

_____

_____

- -

Write letters for 🐴 or a to finish the words in the box.
Use ore, our or au. Finish the sentences with these words.

m_____

_____

bec____se

_____

Is this _____ corn?

Do you want _____ _____ balls?

His arm is sore _____ he

had a fall.

- -

Circle the correct word for each clue.

the side of a room   – call   wall   tall

a number   – your   four

part of your head   – saw   paw   jaw

you put this in a bottle   – cork   fork   pork

you eat this   – torn   horn   corn

 v ve   🏺 vase   👘 sleeve

List Words

| vet | give | love | eleven |
| vest | have | very | twelve |

Letters	Words

1 **Underline** the letter or letters for 🏺 v ve in each List Word. If any of these are not in the sound box, write them with a word example in the box above.

2 **Colour** the vase **blue** if you hear 🏺 v ve at the **start** of the picture name.
Colour the vase **orange** if you hear 🏺 v ve at the **end** of the picture name.

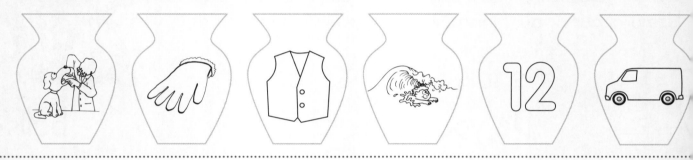

3 **Write** v or ve to finish the words in the box. **Finish** the sentences with these words.

___et   gi___
___est   lo___
___ery   ha___

The _____ has a _____.
I _____ a _____ big van.
I _____ to _____ gifts.

4 **Unjumble** the letters to make a number word.
Draw this many flowers in the vase.

evfi   eeelnv   lveetw

w wh u

 web   whale   queen

st Words				Letters	Words
vas	when	twin	water		
vhat	why	swim	queen		

Underline the letter or letters for w wh u in each List Word. If any of these are not in the sound box, write them with a word example in the box above.

Where do you hear w wh u in the picture name? **Colour** the drop **blue** if it is **first** and **yellow** if it is **second**. **Finish** the words to match the pictures.

w___ns   ___ater   twel___   ___atch   q___een

Write the letters in the drops to finish the words. **Finish** the sentences with these words.

sw	___im ___eep	I _____ in the water.
tw	___in ___elve	Wally has a _____.
qu	___ick ___een	The _____ was wet.

Write Was, Why, What, When to finish the questions.

_____ is the spider's web wet?

_____ did it rain?

_____ it raining last night?

_____ happened to the spider?

For the Extra Challenge turn to page 83.

 **oo u** **book**  **bush**

List Words				Letters	Words
book	good	put	putting		
look	wood	push	pulling		
took	foot	pull	would		
cook	stood	bull	could		

1 Underline the letter or letters for  in each List Word. If any of these are not in the sound box, write them with a word example in the box above.

2 Colour the book if you hear  in the picture name.

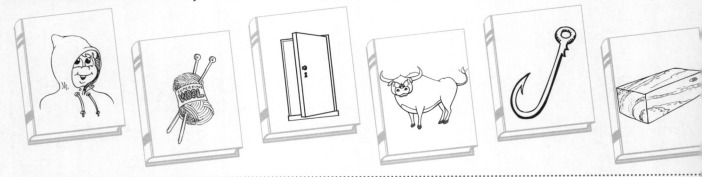

3 Write oo to finish the words. **Join** the pictures to the correct words.

★ We sometimes write **oo** for , as in b**oo**k .

b___k   g___d   t___k   f___t

c___k   w___d   l___k   st___d

4 Put a cross on the picture and the word if you cannot hear the  sound. The first one is done for you.

balloon   hood   moon   hook   broom   roof

Write u to finish the words. **Write** one of your words for each picture.

★ We sometimes write **u** for (**oo u**), as in b**u**sh.

f___ll   p___sh   p___t   b___ll   b___sh

p___lling   p___shing   p___tting

_____   _____   _____

Finish the sentences with words from the books.
Write yes or **no** to answer the questions.

Could book

_____ a bull read a _____?

Answer:_____

foot Would

_____ a bull stand on one _____?

Answer:_____

Write oo or **u** to finish the words.
Colour oo parts **yellow**.
Colour u parts **red**.

Who would wear this –
a **chook**,
a **cook**
or
a **crook**?

Answer: _____

l___k   b___k

p___lling   sh___k

                h___k

b___ll

      p___sh   w___l

      p___t

t___k   c___k   w___d

For the Extra Challenge turn to page 83.

y **yoyo**

List Words

yap	yells	yoyo	you
yet	yelled	year	your
yes	yelling	yard	yolk
yell	yellow	yawn	yabby

Letters	Words

1 Underline the letter or letters for **y** in each List Word. If any of these are not in the sound box, write them with a word example in the box above.

2 Colour the yoyo if you hear **y** in the picture name.

3 Count the sounds in each picture name. **Write** this number in the yoyo string loop. **Join** the words to the pictures.

yabby   yolk   yoghurt   yoyo   yawn

4 Write List Words to match these clues.

This is a colour. _____

This word is the opposite of no. _____

This is space outside, around a house. _____

This word has ear in it. _____

Write y or Y in the spaces.
Read the sentences. Colour the picture.

__olly is a __abby.

__olly has a __o__o.

Write y in the words in the boxes. Finish the sentences with these words.

__ell
__ells
__elled
__elling

Someone is _____.

Did you _____ in the yard?

I _____ out to my friend.

He _____ if he sees a yabby.

__ou
__our

_____ yoyo is yellow.

Can _____ use the yoyo?

Count the sounds in the words. Write the letter or letters for each sound in a separate box. The first one is done for you.

yell	y	e	ll
yet			
you			

yap			
yawn			
yard			

For the Extra Challenge turn to page 83.   ISBN 978 1 74135 156 9

Unit 29

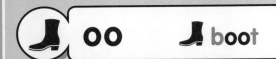 oo    boot

List Words

do	two	food	you
to	too	room	flew
into	moon	cool	new
who	boot	noon	knew

Letters   Words

1 Underline the letter or letters for 🥾oo in each List Word. If any of these are not in the sound box, write them with a word example in the box above.

2 Colour the boot if you hear 🥾oo in the picture name. **Write** a stroke in the top of the boot for each sound in the picture name. The first one is done for you.

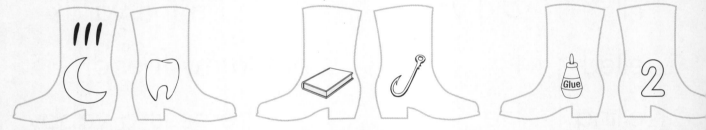

3 Write oo to finish the words. **Join** the pictures to the correct words.

★ We sometimes write oo for 🥾oo , as in boot 🥾.

t____   c____l   m____n 🌙   t____th

b____t   f____d   r____m 🦷   n____n

4 Write to, two or too in the sentences.
Draw Sue and Tom at school.

Sue has _____ boots.

She wears her boots _____ school.

Tom wear boots _____ .

Underline the letter or letters for 🥾 oo in the words in the box.
Finish the sentences with these words.

do	few
into	new
you	knew

I have _____ boots.

We went _____ the room.

I _____ you could _____ it.

A _____ of us will help _____.

Write **Who** to start each question. **Answer** the questions with words from the box.

_____ says moo?   _____

_____ lives in a zoo?   _____

_____ makes food?   _____

_____ has one tooth?   _____

| cook |
| cow |
| baby |
| monkey |

Help Sue find her blue boot.
Colour 🥾 oo parts **blue**.
Colour 📖 oo u parts **red**.

Where would Sue
keep her boots –
in her **pool**,
in her **room**
or
on her **roof** ?

Answer: _____

look   good
        hook   took
moon
    put   spoon   food
                        cook
        wool   cool
            moo
                        wood
    hood

For the Extra Challenge turn to page 83.   ISBN 978 1 74135 156 9

 **z zz s**   **zebra**    **puzzle**   **bears**

List Words				Letters	Words
is	zoo	zoom	fizz		
his	zip	quiz	buzz		
as	zero	prize	buzzing		
was	does	zebra	puzzle		

1 **Underline** the letter or letters for  **z zz s** in each List Word. If any of these are not in the sound box, write them with a word example in the box above.

2 **Colour** the picture if you hear **z zz s** in the picture name. **Write** a stroke below the picture for each sound in the picture name, like this: *zip* /z/i/p/ **III**.

         ↓ 0 1 2 3

_____   _____   _____   _____   _____

3 **Write** z, zz, s or Z to finish the words. **Read** the poem. **Draw** the picture.

___oe i___ a ___ebra,

Striped black and white.

___oe play___ with pu___le___,

And a bu___ing kite.

Write List Words to rhyme with these words.
Colour the letters for **z zz s** in each word.

has	you	room	his
			f

cries	hero	buzz	is
			q

Count the sounds in the words. **Write** the letter or letters for each sound in a separate box. The first one is done for you.

zoom	z	oo	m	
was				
quiz				
zero				
does				

 s si  **treasure**  **television**

What sound do you hear after  **e** in 🗝? Say this sound every time you see **s si**.

Colour the picture if you hear **s si** in the picture name.
Colour the letters for **s si** in the words for these pictures.

treasure

measure

present

noise

television

For the Extra Challenge turn to page 83 .

 **ou ow**  cloud ⚘ **flower**

List Words

how	our	town	about
now	out	down	round

Letters **Words**

1 **Underline** the letter or letters for 🌥 ou ow in each List Word. If any of these are not in the sound box, write them with a word example in the box above.

2 **Colour** the cloud if you hear 🌥 ou ow in the picture name.
Write a stroke beside the cloud for each sound in the picture name.

3 **Write** **ow** to finish the words. **Join** the pictures to the correct words.

★ We sometimes write **ow** for 🌥 ou ow, as in fl**ow**er ⚘.

c____ 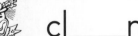   d____n

h____   cl____n

4 **Write** **ou** to finish the words. **Join** the pictures to the correct words.

★ We sometimes write **ou** for 🌥 ou ow, as in cl**ou**d ☁.

____t    h____se

____r   m____se

5 **Write** words from the brackets to finish the sentences.

We came _____ of _____ house.   [ou / our

_____ do you go to town _____ ?   [now / How

I went _____ the hill to the _____ .   [dow... / tow...

I am _____ to go _____ the hill.   [roun... / abo...

▶ For the Extra Challenge turn to page

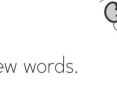

List Words

cake	kite	note	cube
ape	bite	cone	tube

Say the words. **Write** e in the spaces to make new words.
Join the words to the pictures.

tap___   can___   cap___   kit___   hid___

pip___   rid___   not___   rob___   tub___

Write letters to finish the words. **Use** a_e, i_e, o_e or u_e.

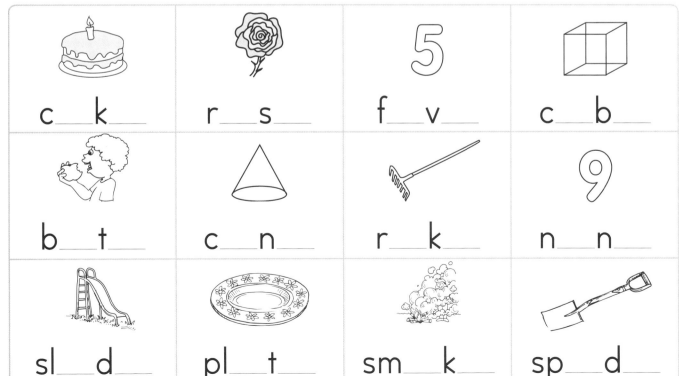

c__k__	r__s__	f__v__	c__b__
b__t__	c__n__	r__k__	n__n__
sl__d__	pl__t__	sm__k__	sp__d__

 **ch**   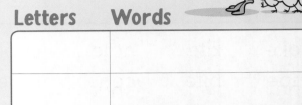 **chicken**

List Words

chip	much	beach	church
chop	which	chain	lunch

Letters	Words

1 **Underline** the letter or letters for ch in each List Word. If any of these are not in the sound box, write them with a word example in the box above.

2 **Colour** the chicken **yellow** if you hear ch at the **start** of the picture name. **Colour** the chicken **orange** if you hear ch at the **end** of the picture name

3 **Finish** the words to match the pictures.

 bea___   l__nch   ch__ps

4 **Count** the sounds in the words. **Write** the letter or letters for each sound in a separate box. The first one is done for you.

much	m	u	ch
chop			

which			
chain			

5 **Write** List Words to match the clues.

This is a good place on a hot day. _____

We eat this in the middle of the day. _____

Some people pray here. _____

sh 🐚 shell

List Words

ship	fish	shelf	push
shell	wish	shark	wash

Letters   **Words**

Underline the letter or letters for 🐚 sh in each List Word. If any of these are not in the sound box, write them with a word example in the box above.

Colour the shell **pink** if you hear 🐚 sh at the **start** of the picture name.
Colour the shell **purple** if you hear 🐚 sh at the **end** of the picture name.

Count the sounds in each picture name. **Write** this number on the line.
Finish the words to match the pictures.

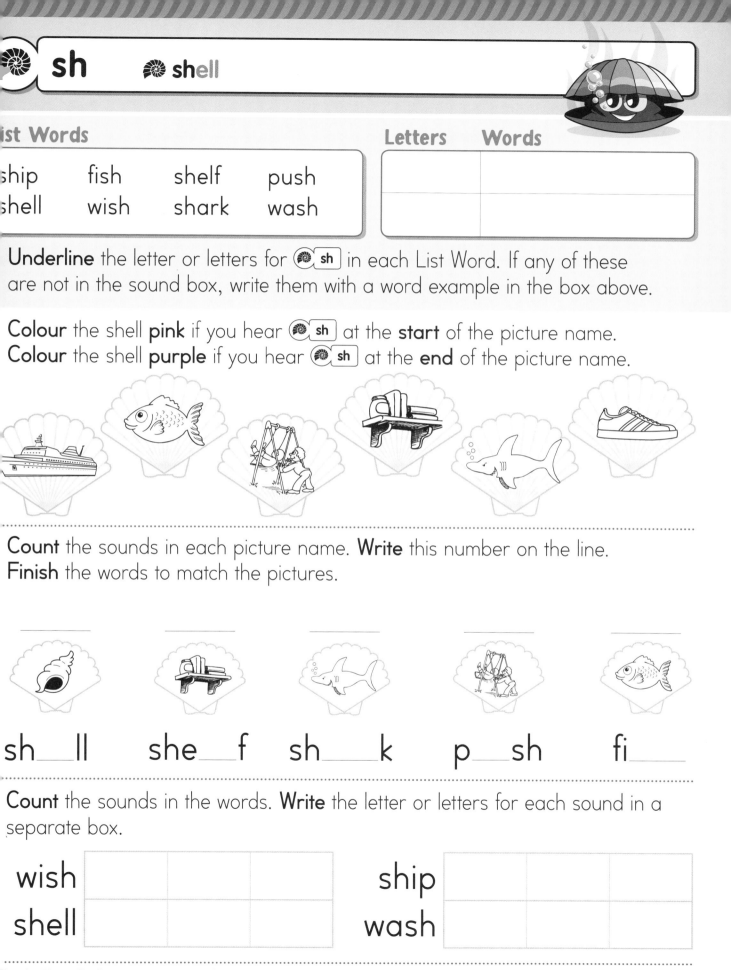

sh___ll   she___f   sh___k   p___sh   fi___

Count the sounds in the words. **Write** the letter or letters for each sound in a separate box.

wish			
shell			

ship			
wash			

For the Extra Challenge turn to page 83.   ISBN 978 1 74135 156 9

 **oy oi**  **boy** **coin**

List Words

toy	boy	oil	coin
toys	boys	oils	join

Letters   Words

1 **Underline** the letter or letters for  **oy oi** in each List Word. If any of these are not in the sound box, write them with a word example in the box above.

2 **Colour** the boy if you hear **oy oi** in the picture name.

3 **Make** real words with the letters the boys are holding.

4 **Write** oy in these words then draw.   **Write** oi in these words then draw.

The b___s
have t___s.

These c___ns
all j___n.

eer ear    d**eer**   ear

ist Words

ear	hear	fear	dear
year	here	near	deer

Letters   **Words**

Underline the letter or letters for  eer ear in each List Word. If any of these are not in the sound box, write them with a word example in the box above.

Say the picture name. **Colour** one deer for every sound you hear.

Write hear and **here** to finish the sentences.
★ You **hear** with your *ear.* **Here** means *where.*

Can you _____ me?

Come over _____.

_____ is the boy with the toys.

I can _____ the bird.

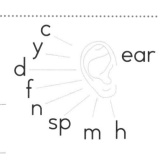

Make real words with the letters around the ear.

_____   _____   _____

c
y
d
f
n
sp   m   h
ear

 th    thong

List Words

thin	thing	three	bath
thick	think	with	path

Letters **Words**

1 Underline the letter or letters for th in each List Word. If any of these are not in the sound box, write them with a word example in the box above.

2 Colour the thong **orange** if you hear th at the **start** of the picture name. **Colour** the thong **yellow** if you hear th at the **end** of the picture name.

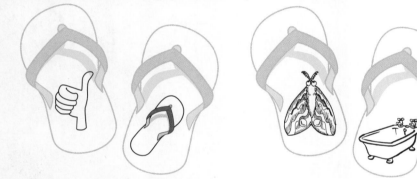

3 Finish the words to match the pictures.

 t___th   3 th__ee   __ath

 tee___   tho__s   p__th

4 Write words from the brackets to finish the sentence.

A _____ snake is on the _____ .   [path / thin

I _____ I will read this _____ book.   [think / thick

I will take that _____ _____ me.   [with / thing

st Words

he	then	they	there
hat	them	these	their

Letters   **Words**

Underline the letter or letters for ✎ th in each List Word. If any of these are not in the sound box, write them with a word example in the box above.

Count the sounds in the words. **Write** the letter or letters for each sound in a separate box.

this

that

them

there

Unjumble these List Words.

tneh   _____n   yteh   _____y

eehts   _____e   rieht   _____r

Finish the sentences with **Their** or **There**.
Read the sentences. **Draw** a picture.
★ **There** means *where*. **Their** means *belonging to them*.

_____ are the boys.

They are on the path.

_____ feet are dirty.

They need a bath.

For the Extra Challenge turn to page 83.   ISBN 978 1 74135 156 9   Sound Waves 1 Student Book

List Words

hair	air	chair	their
pair	stairs	where	there

Letters   Words

1 **Underline** the letter or letters for  **air** in each List Word. If any of these are not in the sound box, write them with a word example in the box above.

2 **Colour** the chair if you hear **air** in the picture name. **Write** a stroke on the line for each sound in the picture name.

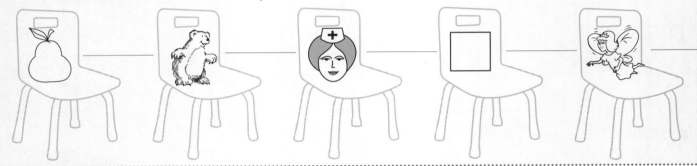

3 **Make** real words with the letters around the chair.

_____   _____

_____   _____

h
p
g   air
f
ch   dr

4 **Finish** the sentences with **their**, **there** or **where**.

★ **There** means *where*. **Their** means *belonging to them*.

Put the chair _____.

_____ hair is fair.

_____ did you put _____ toys?

_____ toys are _____ on the stairs.

▶ For the Extra Challenge turn to page

ist Words

plant	truck	skate	plane
clock	stamp	grape	twenty

Finish the words to match the pictures.

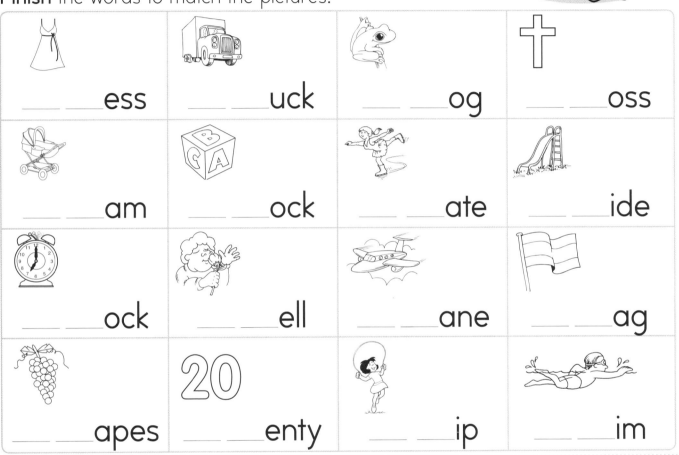

_____ess	_____uck	_____og	_____oss
_____am	_____ock	_____ate	_____ide
_____ock	_____ell	_____ane	_____ag
_____apes	_____enty	_____ip	_____im

Finish the words to match the pictures.

de_____	ma_____	te_____	be_____
wi_____	mi_____	pla_____	sta_____

 er    ladd**er**

List Words

ever	under	better	mother
over	other	letter	father

Letters   Words

1 **Underline** the letter or letters for  er in each List Word. If any of these are not in the sound box, write them with a word example in the box above.

2 **Colour** the picture if you hear  er in the picture name. **Colour** one rung on the ladder for each sound you hear in the picture name.

3 **Write** er to finish the words. **Join** the pictures to the correct words.

★ We sometimes write **er** for  er , as in ladd**er** .

jump____   nev____   bett____

lett____   fath____   moth____

4 **Write** er to finish the words in the box. **Finish** the sentences with these words.

oth____

und____

ev____

ov____

This is my _____ brother.

Did you _____ get my letter

Did you go _____ or

_____ the ladder?

▶ For the Extra Challenge turn to page

Revision

 ar a   ir ur   or a

List Words

star	park	turn	short
dart	pork	torn	shirt

Write **ar**, **ir**, **or** or **ur** to finish the words. **Count** the sounds in each word.
Colour pictures with **2** sounds **red**, **3** sounds **purple** and **4** sounds **blue**.

sh___t	h___n	c___	d___t
b___n	st___	t___n	th___ty
p___k	f___st	t___n	t___ch

Count the number of sounds in each word. **Colour** the shapes.

Colour shapes with –
1 sound word **purple**
2 sound words **red**
3 sound words **blue**
4 sound words **green**.

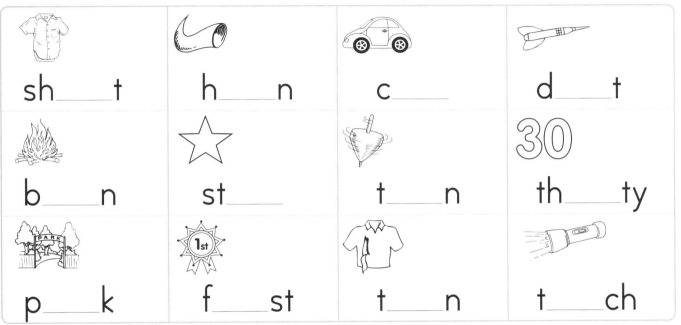

her   or   car   turn   arm   ear   park   were
fur   call   thirty   two   corn
start   first
other
coin   last   slide   star
art   snail   more
saw   shark   fork   your
are   far   air   for

CATERPILLAR CHECK UP

Read your way through the caterpillars.

Consonant Sounds

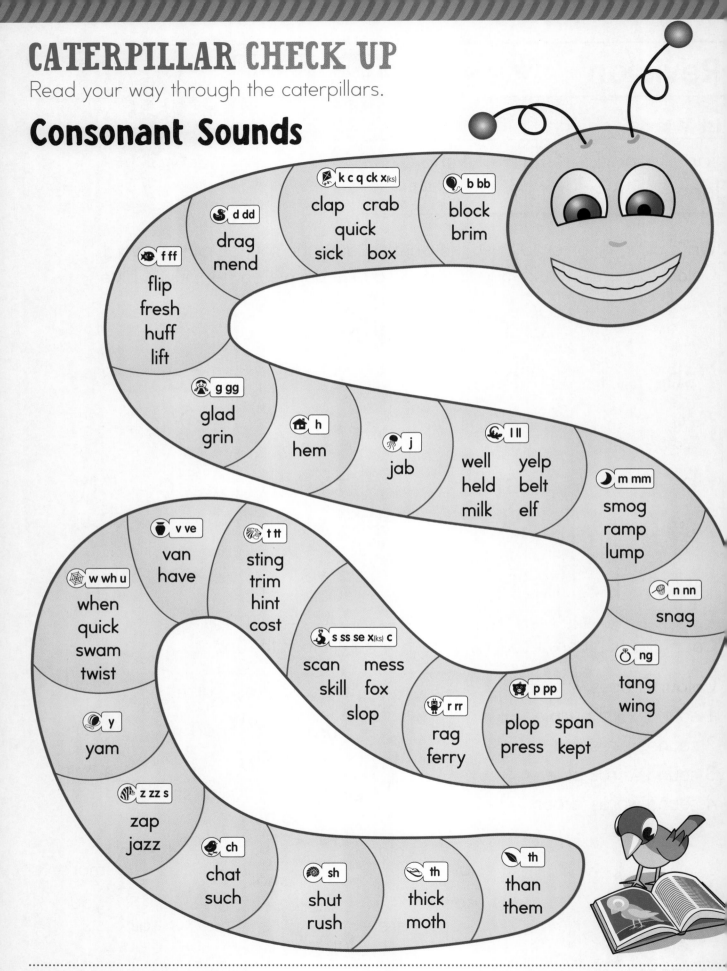

Vowel Sounds

Teachers

Have the student read the words on the caterpillars. If the student is able to decode the word, record a ✓. Instant recognition is not expected. If the student is not yet able to decode the word, record a •.

Students can also be asked to write the words in a written test to assess their ability to encode the words.

Reading and writing the words on the caterpillars requires students to demonstrate the skills that are the major focus of each unit.

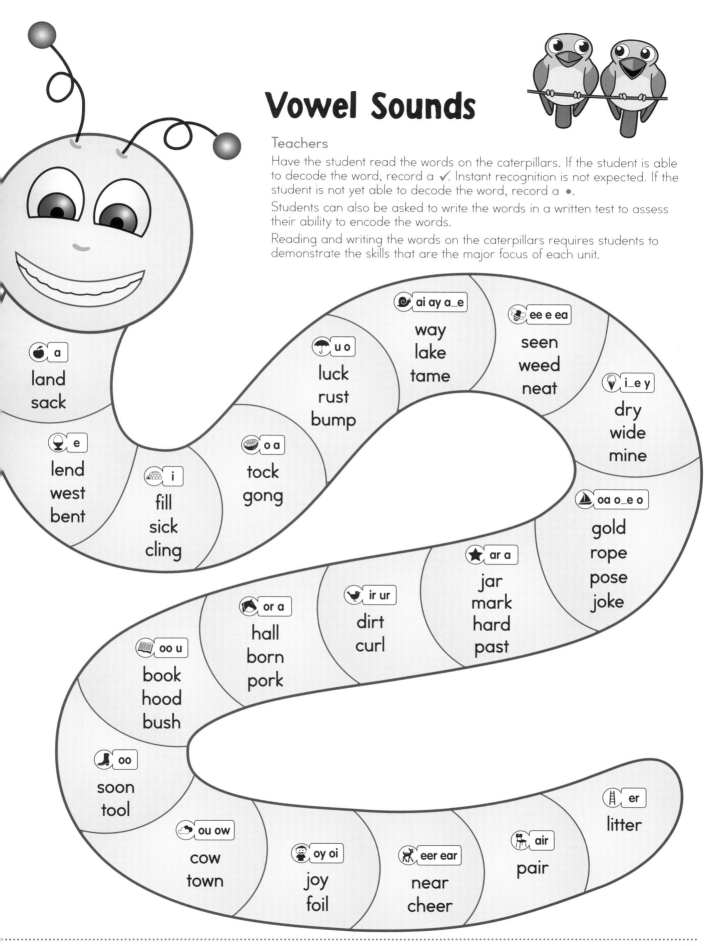

a
land
sack

e
lend
west
bent

i
fill
sick
cling

o a
tock
gong

u o
luck
rust
bump

ai ay a_e
way
lake
tame

ee e ea
seen
weed
neat

i_e y
dry
wide
mine

oa o_e o
gold
rope
pose
joke

ar a
jar
mark
hard
past

ir ur
dirt
curl

or a
hall
born
pork

oo u
book
hood
bush

oo
soon
tool

ou ow
cow
town

oy oi
joy
foil

eer ear
near
cheer

air
pair

er
litter

Consonant Sounds

b bb	before	blow	broom	bubble
balloon	believe	bread	brother	busy
ribbon	birthday	break	brought	rabbit
	blank	breakfast	brown	ribbon

k c q ck x(ks)	across	clipped	fixed	quickly
kite sock	boxes	creep	kissing	quiet
car fox	bucket	cricket	kitten	struck
queen	cliff	excited	next	tricky

d dd	cuddle	dollar	drink	second
duck	dance	dragon	middle	sound
paddle	died	draw	paddle	spend
	different	dream	riddle	suddenly

f ff	cliff	flame	fright	laugh
fish	dolphin	flavour	frost	photo
cliff	drift	float	fruit	stuff
	elephant	flower	giraffe	telephone

g gg	again	forgot	goodbye	ground
girl	begged	garden	great	grow
egg	begging	glass	green	together
	dragging	glove	grey	wiggle

h	happen	head	helped	hottest
house	happy	healthy	high	hundred
	hasn't	heard	hitting	whole
	haven't	heavy	horse	whose

j	cage	giant	jigsaw	juggle
jellyfish	change	jacket	join	jungle
	enjoy	jeans	jolt	junk
	gentle	jetty	juice	stage

l ll	always	fellow	laughing	silk
lizard	animal	felt	lovely	smelt
bell	balloon	later	shall	sulk
	built	learn	shelf	yelp

m mm	climb	money	remember	stump
moon	cramp	morning	smart	summer
hammer	lamb	music	smoke	swam
	mail	number	smooth	swimmer

n nn	funny	know	November	snow
net	join	money	planning	spinning
winner	knee	ninety	snail	winner
	knife	noise	sneeze	winning

ng	along	hanging	spring	thank
ring	belong	hungry	sting	thinking
	drank	kangaroo	strong	wrong
	drink	singer	swing	young

p pp	apple	planet	price	space
pig	happy	plant	princess	spend
slipper	people	please	prize	spider
	picture	popping	puppet	sport

r rr	cherries	raining	rocket	worry
robot	fry	receive	rough	write
carrot	hurry	remember	strawberry	writing
	marry	river	tomorrow	wrong

s ss se x(ks) c	centre	fence	nurse	skirt
seal fox	chance	glass	sauce	sleeve
kiss pencil	circle	grass	scare	slippery
mouse	city	horse	sister	slowly

t tt	button	plant	station	toast
tiger	crust	pretty	street	tonight
button	front	spent	television	travel
	kitten	stairs	terrible	trust

v ve	above	favourite	lovely	vehicle
vase	diver	giving	move	video
sleeve	every	haven't	river	visitor
	everyone	leave	travel	voice

w wh u	quarter	squeeze	twinkle	while
web	question	swept	twisting	window
whale	quickly	swift	welcome	winter
queen	quilted	twenty	whale	women

y	yummy	using	yearly	young
yoyo	huge	usually	yesterday	youngest
	human	yacht	yoga	yours
	used	yawn	yoghurt	yourself

z zz s	always	goes	size	zebra
zebra	busy	please	sizzle	zest
puzzle	close	present	sneeze	zone
bears	closing	quizzes	squeeze	zooming

s si			
treasure	**Teacher's Note:** The s as in treasure is
television	formally introduced in *Sound Waves 4*.

ch	catch	chew	kitchen	reach
chicken	change	children	match	stretch
	chases	crunch	peaches	such
	cheese	itch	picture	teaches

sh	finish	shelves	short	special
shell	polish	shiny	shouldn't	splash
	rubbish	shiver	shout	squash
	selfish	shoe	shower	sugar

th	birthday	teeth	thorn	thunder
thong	month	thank	threw	Thursday
	mouth	third	throw	truth
	something	thirsty	thumb	without

th	brother	gather	they'll	though
feather	clothes	rather	they're	together
	either	smooth	they've	weather
	feather	that's	those	whether

a apple	angry animal answer apple	carry catch dance dragged	hang happen happy packet	planning Saturday stamp thank

e egg	anything bread breakfast fellow	forever friend head letter	many present ready second	seventeen spent swept twenty

i igloo	anything children different dripping	fifteen finish inside kitten	misses picture pretty quickly	sister stick thicker winter

o a orange watch	along anybody block dolphin	follow gone holiday knock	often orange pocket softly	stopping strong wander wasn't

u o umbrella monkey	above bunch colour coming	country crust hundred money	none number other running	shutting someone summer trunk

ai ay a_e snail hay cake	afraid baby break danger	eighteen great holiday ladies	paper plate snake space	strange table train yesterday

ee e ea bee me seat	already anybody babies cheese	easy green lady metre	please quickly reach street	suddenly teacher these twenty

i_e y ice-cream fly	behind bright cries eye	fright ice-cream library ninety	shine shiny slide slime	tonight white why write

oa o_e o boat rose comb	both close clothes don't	float flow known ocean	only open show stone	those throw tomorrow window

ar a star glass	afternoon aren't asked asking	banana basket carpet class	garden laugh mask party	past spark start tomato

ir ur bird nurse	birthday burnt certain circus	early earth furniture heard	learn nurse purple purse	Thursday turned weren't world

or a horse ball	always bought brought caught	draw football horse quarter	sport storm straw talking	warm worn you're yourself

oo u book bush	butcher cookbook couldn't crook	football footpath goodbye pulled	pushed pushing shook should	soot sugar woman wouldn't

oo boot	balloon blew broom classroom	flew grew juice school	spoon threw through true	Tuesday use used using

ou ow cloud flower	amount cloud clown count	crowd crown flower frown	ground loud mountain mouth	shout sound thousand towel

oy oi boy coin	annoy boil choice destroy	enjoy joy noise noisy	oyster point poison royal	soil spoil toilet voice

eer ear deer ear	appear beard beer cereal	cheer cheering clear cleared	disappear feared nearly rear	shear shearing spear steer

air chair	anywhere bare bear care	careful dare downstairs fair	repair scare scary spare	square stare upstairs wear

er ladder	animal brother butter children	circus corner dinner doctor	dollar farmer letter paper	pizza sister summer winter

as for using Extension Word Lists

d the Words: Read the words in the list for the sound being lied, saying the word then segmenting the word into its sounds, example *cloud |c||l|ou|d|*.

d a Word: Read the list for the sound being studied. Play *Find a Word*, example, find a word that is an animal. Find a word that ends with  er .

go: Students select 8 words from the list being studied and write the ds down. Teacher calls out the words to be covered. Winner is the first over 4 in a row.

Super Challenge: Select a difficult word of the day or week to learn to spell. Display prominently. Test the class at the end of the day/week.

Find the Grapheme: Find the different spelling choices for the sound being studied.

Sort Words: Sort words according to the number of sounds or the graphemes representing the focus sound.

Column Challenge: Select a column of 4 words for the sound being studied. Challenge the students to write a sensible sentence containing all 4 words.

EXTRA CHALLENGES

Unit 2
b bb

Find words with **b**, **br**, **bl**, **bb** or **B** in reading books. Write a **b** list, a **br** list, a **bl** list, a **bb** list and a **B** list.

Unit 3
a

Draw a big apple tree on a piece of paper. Fill the tree with words that rhyme with *cat*, *hand* and *back*.

Unit 4
k c q ck x (ks)

Make a k c q ck x (ks) picture and word booklet for younger children.

Unit 5
e

Draw more eggs and fill them with the jumbled letters of e words as in Activity 7 on page 15.

Unit 6
d dd

On a card, draw a big duck. Inside, draw pictures of things with d dd in their names. Colour it neatly. Cut into 4 or 5 pieces to make a jigsaw. Give it to a friend to put back together.

Unit 7
i

Draw an igloo made of blocks and fill it with i words.

Unit 8
f ff

Draw some large fish on cards. Draw an **f**, **ff**, **fr**, **fl** and **F** picture in each one. Write the word for each picture underneath. Cut them out. Put a paper clip on each fish. Play *Fish* using magnets on string.

Unit 9
o a

Draw 2 orange trees. Put words with the letter **o** for o a on one and the letter **a** for o a on the other.

Unit 10
g gg

Draw 5 things starting with g gg that you could give to a girl as a gift, for example *gloves*.

Unit 11
u o

Fold a piece of paper into 4 parts. Draw these things and label: a pup in a cup, a duck in a truck, a bug on a rug, Mum with a drum.

Unit 12
h
j

Draw a house that a jellyfish could live in under the sea. Draw h things and j things in the house.

Unit 13
ai ay a_e

Draw a chain of 10 snails. Write an ai ay a_e word on each snail.

Unit 14
l ll

Draw a big lizard on card. Fill the lizard with pattern using straight lines. Colour your patte

Unit 15
ee e ea

Go on a sound or phoneme hunt in reading books. Find as many words as possible with ee e ea in them.

Unit 16
m mm

Write 3 silly sentences about the moon. Use List Words in each sentence. For examp *Mummy is swimming on the moon*. Draw a picture for each sentence.

Unit 17
i_e y

Draw 3 big ice-creams and fill them with wor that rhyme with *nine*, *ride* and *five*.

Unit 18
n nn
ng

How many words on pages 40 and 41 can y find that have 3 sounds in them? Make a list. Show a friend.

Unit 19
oa o_e o

Draw 3 colourful sailing boats. Put *old* on one sail, *nose* on another and *joke* on the thi Write rhyming words on each boat.

t 20 [pp] [r]	Fold a piece of paper into 8 rectangles. Write a List Word in each rectangle. Play *Bingo* with your teacher.	**Unit 29** [oo]	Draw a large boot and fill with [oo] words. Draw a large book and fill with [oo u] words.
t 21 [a]	Cut out star shapes. Put a different [ar a] word on each one. Hang the stars as a mobile.	**Unit 30** [z zz s]	Jumble the letters of some List Words. Give to a friend to unjumble.
t 22 [s se x(ks) c]	With play dough or plasticine, make Sid the mouse and his friend the fox. Write and illustrate a story about them.	**Unit 31** [ou ow]	Write sentences that contain 3 or 4 List Words. For example: *Our cow went round the town.* Draw a picture for each sentence.
t 23 [ur]	Write questions about birds starting with *were*. For example: *Were the birds in the surf?*	**Unit 32** [ch] [sh]	Choose 10 words from the [ch] and [sh] List Words. Think of a rhyming word for each one. Write all your words on separate cards. Play *Snap* or *Match Up* with your friends.
t 24 [ ]	Draw a large tent and a large nest on a piece of paper. Write words to rhyme with *tent* on the tent and write words to rhyme with *nest* on the nest.	**Unit 33** [oy oi] [eer ear]	Write a sentence about a boy and toys. For example: *That boy has too many toys.* Draw a picture for it. Write a sentence about a deer and ears. For example: *I saw a deer with very long ears.* Draw a picture for it.
t 25 [a]	Read the sentences in Activity 4 on page 54. Draw the things we saw on our walk.	**Unit 34** [th] [th]	In a large thong shape, write all the [th] List Words. In a large feather shape write all the [th] List Words.
t 26 [ve] [wh u]	Draw 5 vases on a sheet of paper. Write the words for 6, 7, 8, 9 and 10 on the vases, writing one number word on each vase. Draw that many flowers on each vase.	**Unit 35** [air]	Write some *where* questions about bears, fairies, chairs and stairs. For example: *Where are the chairs for the bears?*
t 27 [u]	Make a bookmark. Cut a strip of cardboard and write *bookmark* on it in large print. Decorate.	**Unit 36** [er]	Draw other people and things that have [er] on the end of their names.
t 28 [ ]	Write some questions that will have 'yes' for the answer. For example: *Does a yoyo have a string?* Remember to put a question mark at the end of the question.		

HELPFUL HINTS

Teachers can use this information to help with spelling.

1 Adding ed and ing to words with a **CVC** pattern

[1] To add to words with a **CVC** pattern, we often double the last letter if it comes straight after the letters **a, e, i, o, u** for [a], [e], [i], [oa] or [uo] before the ending is added, for example *rubbed/rubbing*.

2 Adding ed and ing to words with a **CVCC** pattern

[2] To add to words with a **CVCC** pattern, we usually do not double the last letter, because it is **not** straight after any of the letters **a, e, i, o, u** for [a], [e], [i], [oa] or [uo], for example *jumped/jumping*.

3 Adding ed and ing to words ending with **e**

[3a] To add **ed**, we usually leave the **e** and just add **d**, for example *placed, liked*.

[3b] To add **ing**, we usually take off the **e** before we add **ing**, for example *having, placing*.

4 Using k, c, ck, x

[4a] We often write **k** for [k c q ck x(ks)] at the start of words, if the next letter is **e** or **i**, for example *kick, kettle*. With other letters, we usually write **c**, for example *cat, cry, cup, cot*.   Introduced Ur

[4b] The letter **c** often represents [s ss se x(ks) c] when it is followed by **e, i** or **y**, for example *cent, city, lacy*.   Introduced Unit

[4c] We often write **ck** for [k c q ck x(ks)] straight after the letters **a, e, i, o, u** for [a], [e], [i], [oa], [uo] for example *back, check, kick, lock, luck*. After other sounds we often write **k**, for example *peak, bake, book, work, park, pink*.   Introduced Ur

[4d] We can write **x** for the blend of two sounds [k c q ck x(ks)], [s ss se x(ks) c], for example *six, box*.   Introduced Ur

5 Using ff, ll, ss, zz

[5a] We often use **ff, ll, ss, zz** on the end of words, straight after the letters **a, e, i, o, u** for [a], [e], [i], [oa] or [uo], for example *puff, bell, kiss, fizz*.   Introduced Ur

6 Using vowel sounds after [w wh u]

[6a] We often write **a** for [oa] after [w wh u], for example *watch, was, what*.   Introduced Ur

[6b] We often write **or** for [ir ur] after [w wh u], for example *work, word*.   Introduced Unit

7 Using vowel sounds on the end of words

[7a] We usually write **ay** for [ai ay a_e] on the end of words, for example *day, pay*.   Introduced Unit

[7b] We usually write **oy** for [oy oi] on the end of words, for example *boy, toy*.   Introduced Unit

8 Using ve on the end of words

[8] We usually write **ve** for [v ve] on the end of a word, for example *give, have, sleeve*.   Introduced Unit

9 Homophones

[9] Homophones are words that sound the same but have different spelling, for example *knows/nose, to/too/two, hear/here, there/their*.   Introduced Unit